Dedicated to all the children around the world.
No matter what, be grateful.

Prolance

www.prolancewriting.com
California, USA
© 2022 Halimah Bashir

ISBN: 978-1-7371558-0-5

A SENSE of GRATITUDE

EXPLORING
THE
FIVE SENSES

Written by Halimah Bashir
Illustrated by Laila Ramadhani

PROLANCE

Note to Grown-ups

Raising children is hard work that requires loads of love, patience and prayer. We want to raise children that grow into beautiful, well-rounded, and God-conscious citizens by giving them the tools necessary to thrive in a world riddled with countless distractions and tests. This book was intended to serve as a reminder for all of us to be grateful. My hope is that by exploring the senses we acknowledge the blessings that we often take for granted.

Do we go outdoors and admire the beauty of God's creation? Do we thank God each time we eat? Are we listening to the beautiful recitation of HIS book? It is our responsibility to teach children that all of these senses are interconnected to our spiritual hearts and protecting them is paramount to keeping our hearts clean.

Thank you,
Halimah Bashir

الله has blessed me with
5 senses, I use them everyday.
I am so grateful to الله (God) that He
has made me in such a special way.
Two eyes to see,
a nose to smell,
a tongue so I can taste.
Two hands to touch,
two ears to hear,
on each side of my face.

I use my eyes to enjoy the beauty of
الله (God's) creation.

The mountains, trees, butterflies, bees, the birds flying high in the sky.

The tiny ants that march in a line,
I sit and watch as the time passes by.

The colorful wildflowers
that grow in the forest, so many different kinds.

My eyes can see different colors like
purple, yellow and blue.

Majestic and royal colors like
ruby, gold and silver too.

My nose is placed in the center of my face, it gives me the ability **to smell.**

Sometimes I **whiff**, sometimes I **sniff**, and oftentimes I'll **waft.**

My science teacher tells me **to waft** the chemicals in order to keep safe.

I wave my hands to move **the smell**, wafting slowly towards my face.

I enjoy the **pleasant smells**
like Teta's baked cookies

or **fresh mint** that grows in our garden.

Sometimes I pass by a **not-so-good smell.**
Excuse me, I'm sorry, please pardon.

My tongue is tasked with the important duty
of **tasting things** that are delicious.

Candy, cake and apple
pie, delicious but
not so nutritious.

UGHH....

UGGHH....

Grown–ups tell me to eat
my **fruits and vegetables.**
Some children may be sad.
They don't know I enjoy them all and
secretly I'm glad.

I get tired of sugary sweets and often so does my tummy.

I enjoy the simple things that الله (God) created like apples, cucumbers, carrots and honey.

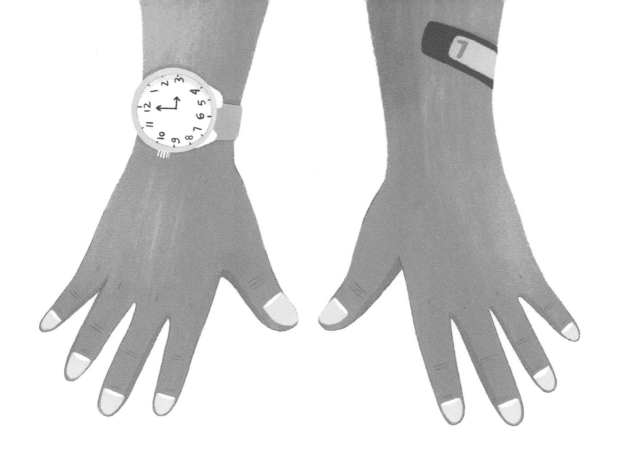

My hands and skin are used to
touch and feel the world around me.

I enjoy a **cozy warm blanket** fresh out the dryer, the best on a cold winter day.

When I'm **not feeling well**, lying sick in bed my loved one is always there.

They **rub my back** and **kiss my head**, showing me that they care.

I use my hands and fingers **to touch**
and hold things I find in nature.
Like slimy frogs

and **hairy dogs,** these things
get me really excited.

My hands are used to **make dua** when I'm happy or feeling blue.

الله (God) tells us **to call on Him** when we are sad and don't know what to do.

My ears, I have two, gifted
to me so I can hear.

ALLAHU AKBAR...

I hear the **sound of the athan.**
hurry up,
it's time to pray!

Honk!
Honk!

VROOM VROOM

I cover my ears as the **firetruck zooms** by.
Don't worry! Help is on the way.

ASSALAMUALAIKUM...

I listen as my Baba's **footsteps** get closer as he walks inside the door.

I feel horrible when I **hear**
my baby brother **start to cry**,
now that I can't ignore.

Two eyes to see,
a nose to smell,
a tongue so I can taste.
Two hands to touch,
Two ears to hear,
on each side of my face.

الله (God) has given us five senses,
We use them everyday.

Thank you الله (God) for creating us all
in such a **special way**.

Glossary:

الله Allah:
Arabic word for the One and only God; Our creator

Dua:
Personal prayer, supplication, To "call out" to God for guidance, help, thanks, and direction

Athan:
A Muslims call to prayer

Baba:
Father; Dad

Teta: Grandmother

Assalamu Alaikum:
An Islamic greeting that means may peace be unto you